VOICES OF EXPERIENCE

Practical Ideas to
Wrap Up the Year

Grades K-3

VOICES OF EXPERIENCE

Practical Ideas to
Wrap Up the Year

Grades K-3

COLLEEN POLITANO • JOY PAQUIN
CAREN CAMERON • KATHLEEN GREGORY

PORTAGE & MAIN PRESS

Portage and Main Press acknowledges the financial support of the Government of Canada through the Book Publishing Industry Development Program (BPIDP) for our publishing activities.

Printed and bound in Canada by Friesens

05 06 07 08 09 5 4 3 2 1

Library and Archives Canada Cataloguing in Publication

Practical ideas to wrap up the year : grades K-3 / Colleen Politano ... [et al.]. (Voices of experience)

Includes bibliographical references.
ISBN 1-55379-032-4

1. Elementary school teaching. I. Politano, Colleen, 1946-
II. Series: Voices of experience (Winnipeg, Man.)

LB1537.P74 2005   372.13   C2005-903158-1

PORTAGE & MAIN PRESS

100-318 McDermot Ave.
Winnipeg, MB Canada R3A 0A2
Email: books@portageandmainpress.com
Tel: 204-987-3500
Toll-free fax: 1-866-734-8477
Toll free: 1-800-667-9673

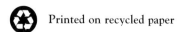 Printed on recycled paper

FOR JOY PAQUIN

In the summer of 2003, the four of us (Caren, Kathleen, Joy, and Colleen) worked together and planned the ideas for all the books in the Voices of Experience series. Shortly before the first two books went to press, Joy died suddenly. The ideas in this series reflect Joy's spirit.

Joy Paquin was a teacher's teacher. She was committed to making classrooms the best places for children and to sharing ideas with others. She was known for her enthusiasm, tireless dedication, and the fun she brought to teaching. Joy did more than teach children to read and write; she taught her students and her friends how to live a full and joyous life. Her professional legacy —one of love, caring, humour, knowledge, and wisdom – will live on for thousands of children, parents, educators, and colleagues.

We dedicate this series to Joy, our dear friend, with love.

Caren, Kathleen, and Colleen

ACKNOWLEDGMENTS

Our sincere thanks to our friends who invited us into their classrooms and shared their ideas, their stories, and their students. We marvel at your dedication to creating classroom communities where all children enjoy being together, feel appreciated for who they are, and become confident, independent learners. You inspire us!

Colleen, Caren, and Kathleen

Contents

Introduction

Who is this series for?

Voices of Experience is a series of six books – three for grades K-3, three for grades 4-8. Each book is full of practical ideas designed for new teachers, teachers new to a grade level, and teachers who want new ideas to reenergize their practice.

What's in the books?

We have compiled our best ideas and organized them into two sets of three books:

- Book 1: for the start of the year when teachers are just getting to know their students

- Book 2: for during the year when teachers need to get themselves and their students "fired up"

- Book 3: for the end of the year when teachers need to wrap things up

Each book is organized into four sections around the acronym ROAR.

R = ideas for building **r**elationships

O = ideas for classroom **o**rganization

A = ideas for classroom **a**ssessment that support student learning

R = ideas that are **r**eliable and ready to use tomorrow

"Create a new model of teacher to teacher support so that every teacher knows every other teacher's best ideas."

— Eric Jensen, Brain-Based Learning

For each idea we provide a brief discussion and easy-to-follow steps. Many also include student examples and unique adaptations. In addition, we have included current information about the brain and how students learn.

We have also included a variety of ways to use this series of books to support professional development activities in different settings; for example, educators' book clubs; team and department meetings and staff meetings; in-service and pre-service workshops; and seminars with student teachers (see appendix A).

Final Note:

The single, most important message we want to leave you with is to listen to your own voice and the voices of your students. Adapt our ideas to fit for you, your students, and your school community.

INTRODUCTION TO RELATIONSHIPS

Establish trust and build relationships before anything else.
Then, place relationships above the rest.

■

Show students you care about them as people,
and let them see you as a person.

■

When relationships are established, students can
take risks and accept new challenges.

■

Emotion is a huge part of the classroom;
it often sets the stage for learning.

■

Relationships: First in the book. First in the classrooms.

In this chapter on relationships, we offer practical
ideas for you and your students to wrap up the
school year. Activities include ways to:

- record memories of the year

- create good wishes for everyone

- celebrate using readers theatre

- write class thank-you letters

- make class songbooks

Yearbook:
recording memories of the year together

DISCUSSION

Take time to "wrap up" the school year together. One way to do this is to have students make class yearbooks. We have our students look back at what they did and learned, and then each person writes about special memories and draws pictures to remember events and people.

Figure 1. Example of student yearbook page

STEPS

1. Talk with students about making a yearbook. We ask our students, "How many people know what a yearbook is? I had a yearbook when I was in school, and I still like to look back and read about my friends and the things we did together. We're going to make a yearbook for our class, so we can record some of our memories from this school year."

2. Print sentence starters for yearbook pages on a piece of chart paper (see figure 2).

3. Give students practice responding orally to the sentence starters. We have each student turn to a partner and take turns telling their responses to each other.

4. Make copies of the black line master on page 55, give each student a copy and ask them to write a response to each sentence starter (see figure 1).

My name is…

My friends are…

My favourite things to do in class are:

I am proud of…

My special memories are…

I'd like to say…

Black line master on p. 55

Figure 2. Sentence starters for yearbook pages

5. Have students meet with a partner to read and talk about their completed yearbook page and make any corrections or additions.

6. Ask students to illustrate their yearbook page (see figure 1).

7. Make a "teacher" page for the beginning of the yearbook and invite other adults in the classroom, such as teaching assistants, to make their own page. On the teacher page we include an introduction for families (see figure 3).

8. Collect and collate the pages of the yearbook and make one complete copy for each student. We make several extra copies to put in the class library.

9. Give students time to read their yearbooks and autograph copies for classmates. This is a special time for our students and we set aside time each day during the last week of school so they can sign autographs.

Dear Families,

This yearbook is a collection of thoughts that capture moments of the school year we spent together.

The children talked and wrote about their ideas and read them to a classmate. I have not made any changes or corrections in the students' work.

It's important to understand that the range of writing that you see in this yearbook is typical of children at this age and stage of development.

We hope you enjoy our yearbook.

Sincerely,
Colleen Politano

Figure 3. Teacher page includes introduction of the yearbook for families.

ADAPTATION

Have younger students complete a yearbook page by drawing and labelling their memories (see figure 4).

Figure 4. Yearbook page completed by a kindergarten student

Good Wishes:
recording "good wishes" to say goodbye to classmates

DISCUSSION

Students remember beginnings and endings. Make the final days of school as memorable as the first days by having students make "good wishes" for each person in the class. We record these wishes and give each student his or her own wish list on the last day of school.

STEPS

1. Tell students they are going to make a wish for each person in the class. We say, "At special times in our lives we make wishes. How many of you make a wish on your birthday? It is almost the end of the school year and next year people may be in different classes. As a way of saying good bye and good luck to each other we are going to make a list of 'good wishes' for each person."

2. Model how to think of and write "good wishes." We think aloud for students and ask them to listen and watch as we record "good wishes" on a large piece of paper. We think of "good wishes" for someone whom everyone in the class knows, such as the principal or secretary. For example, "I am going to write at the top of this paper – 'Good wishes' to the principal. I know he works so hard so I am going to write this good wish for him: *Spend lots of time golfing.*"

3. Ask students if they have any good wishes they would like to add. Record their ideas on the same sheet of paper (see figure 5). We give our students time to have a private "think" about the person before they tell their wishes. We say, "Make a picture in your head of our principal, Mr. Belcher. Think about what he is

good at and what he likes to do. Think about what you might wish for him for this summer, for next year, for his life. What's your wish for Mr. Belcher?"

4. Work together as a class to write "good wishes" for everyone in the classroom, including the teacher and the teaching assistant. We write one or two each day, working in alphabetical order and reassuring students that everyone will receive "good wishes."

5. Store each list of "good wishes" until one has been completed for every student.

6. Give students their own "good wishes" and ask them to design a border. Have the students present their good wishes to the other people in the class, such as the teaching assistant or teacher (see figure 6).

7. Have students read their "good wishes" again before they take them home. We give our students ribbons and show them how to roll up their "good wishes" and tie them to look like a scroll.

Good Wishes to
Mr. Belcher

- Spend lots of time golfing
- Have a good holiday and rest a lot
- Go fishing if you want
- My wish is that you have fun with your friends
- Please come back to our school next year

Figure 5. Class-created "good wishes" for the principal

ADAPTATION

For older students, we post a sheet of paper with one student's name on it, and have students print their "good wishes." Repeat this process until everyone has a "good wishes" list to take home at the end of the year.

Figure 6. Students present the "good wishes" they've written for their teacher.

Celebration Scripts:
using readers theatre
to wrap up the year

DISCUSSION

End the year with a celebration of learning. One way to have students celebrate and share what they have learned during the school year is to have them write and perform a readers theatre script.

STEPS

1. Introduce the idea of readers theatre as a way to wrap up the year. We say, "At this time of year people like to get together to remember the things they've done. One of the ways our class can celebrate our time together is to write and present a readers theatre about our learning and our time together."

2. Record on chart paper an outline for a readers theatre script.

3. Work together with the class to complete the outline of the script. Record the students' ideas on a piece of chart paper (see figure 7).

4. Organize students into small groups and assign a section of the script for each group to practice. We review the basics of readers theatre with our class before they practice reading the celebration script (see figure 8).

5. Give groups time to practice their section of the script.

6. Bring the class together and have them practice reading through the complete script as a whole group.

Figure 7. Outline of readers theatre script completed by the class

This Year

This year we were learners.
Learners who
  • think and plan
  • have our own ideas
  • solve problems
  • like to learn
Learners who will keep on learning!

This year we were friends.
Friends who
  • help each other
  • have fun together
  • share
  • talk and laugh
Friends who will keep on caring!

This year we were readers.
Readers who
  • read lots of books
  • talk about books
  • sound good when we read aloud
  • figure out hard words
Readers who will keep on reading!

This year we were artists.
Artists who
  • sing and dance
  • act and build
  • show the world our way
  • use imagination
Artists who will keep on creating!

7. Have students talk about what worked well and what they need to improve or change. We have students think about their performance and the script, and make any necessary changes.

8. Perform the readers theatre for an audience. We have our students perform at year-end events, and we take the class "on tour" to other classrooms in the school.

ADAPTATION

For older students, make each student a copy of the black line master on page 56, and have them work in groups to write and perform one section of the readers theatre outline (see figure 9).

Readers Theatre Basics

- enter from "stage right" with script under right arm
- turn to face the audience
- make eye contact
- begin with the title
- perform
- bow
- take compliments
- exit "stage left" with script under left arm

Figure 8. Basics of readers theatre

This Year

All: This year we were learners.

Group 1: Learners who
-
-
-
-

Learners who will keep on learning!

Group 2: This year we were friends.
Friends who
-
-
-
-

Friends who will keep on caring!

Group 3: This year were were readers.
Readers who
-
-
-
-

Readers who will keep on reading!

Group 4: This year we were artists.
Artists who
-
-
-
-

Artists who will keep on creating!

Group 5: This year we were mathematicians.
Mathematicians who
-
-
-
-

Mathematicians you can count on!

Group 6: This year we made memories.
Memories of
-
-
-
-

Memories we will always cherish!

Black line master on p. 56

Figure 9. Outline of a script for readers theatre

Thank-you Letters:
taking the time to thank others

"In the early years, the developing limbic system enables the child to form relationships… This is a perfect opportunity to teach children about behaviour toward other people…"

— Carla Hannaford, *Smart Moves*

DISCUSSION

Acknowledging others is a caring and positive way to end the year. Our students write thank-you letters to recognize the people who have helped out in our class. Each letter is framed and personalized with students' illustrations.

STEPS

1. Talk with students about the importance of thanking others. We say, "So many people have helped our class this year to make it better for all of us. I think it's important for us to write some thank-you letters to let these people know how much we have appreciated their support."

2. Ask students to suggest names of people who have helped out in the classroom. Record their suggestions on chart paper and add other names that have not yet been suggested.

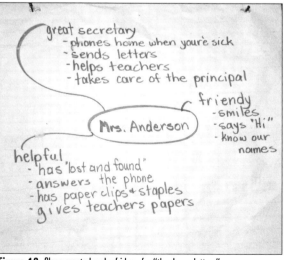

Figure 10. Class-created web of ideas for "thank-you letters"

3. Select one person from the list to write to first. Before writing the class letter, we have our students talk with a partner about what this person did for our class. We record the students' ideas in a web on a piece of chart paper (see figure 10).

4. Work together to compose a collaborative thank-you letter on a piece of chart paper. We ask our students to use the ideas from the web to make the letter specific and personal.

5. Have students decorate the completed letter. We ask each student to draw a picture on a small piece of paper and glue it around the perimeter of the chart paper to form a border (see figure 11).

6. Deliver the thank-you letter. If the person is in the school we invite him or her to come to our class and the students read the letter aloud.

7. Write another thank-you letter to the next person on the list. During the last weeks of school, our class writes at least one thank-you letter per week.

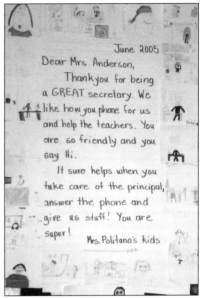

Figure 11. "Thank-you letter" to the school secretary

Class Songbooks:
remembering favourite songs

"Music that you enjoy will cause the release of endorphins – those feel-good brain chemicals."

— Marilee Sprenger,
Learning and Memory

DISCUSSION

Music engages emotions. Have students decide on their "top-ten" songs and make a class songbook for each student to illustrate and keep. We "take requests" in the last week of school to sing our favourite songs one more time as a way to end the year with a positive feeling.

STEPS

1. Talk with students about making a "class songbook." We say, "We are making a songbook so we can remember the words to our favourite songs. As we know so many songs, we need to decide which ones to include in our 'top ten.'"

2. Work together to make a list of songs that the class has learned and record the titles on a piece of chart paper.

3. Decide on a way for students to select their favourite songs. We give each student three stickers and ask them to place these beside the song titles they want to include in the songbook. We tell them they can put all three stickers beside one song or they can put each sticker beside a different song (see figure 12).

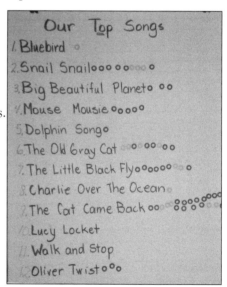

Figure 12. List of favourite songs shown with the most stickers

4. Count the number of stickers beside each song title with the students. Circle the ten songs with the most stickers.

5. Print the words for the selected songs, copy the pages, and collate them into a songbook. We number the songs in the songbook for easy reference.

6. Make copies of the "class songbook" and give one to each student.

7. Ask students to illustrate their songbooks (see figure 13).

8. Set aside time during the last weeks of school to "take requests" to sing favourite songs one more time. As a quick way to decide which song to sing, we put the numbers 1~10 on individual slips of paper, and ask a student to pull a number "out of a hat." We sing the song with the same number as on the slip of paper.

Figure 13. Student-illustrated page of a class songbook

Figure 14. Students place stickers on their favourite songs.

See p. 12

See p. 8

Figure 15. One group reads their part of the year-end "celebration script."

See p. 4

Figure 16. Students sign each other's yearbooks.

INTRODUCTION TO ORGANIZATION

Organize in ways that maximize learning

■

Take time to set up routines and procedures with students;
it saves in the long run.

■

Organize in ways that allow all students to make independent
use of materials, spaces and routines in the classroom.

■

Organization is more than having a neat and tidy classroom.
Organization is about creating a positive,
safe, and orderly environment.

■

The best way to organize is the way that works
best for you and your students.

In this chapter on organization, we offer practical ideas
for you and your students to wrap up the school year.
Activities include ways to:

■ have a career day

■ meet and talk with a partner

■ complete a construction challenge

■ create collaborative pictures as a way to review

■ have the class take a break

Career Day:
experiencing a career for a day

DISCUSSION

Adding novelty at the end of the year can be motivating. We organize our timetable so the class can have a "career day" where they work on activities related to specific careers. This single focus allows students to consolidate their learning and experience a feeling of accomplishment.

STEPS

1. Tell students that the class is going to have a "career day." For example, we say, "You are going to spend an entire day working on the activities that people do in different careers, such as being an athlete, an artist, a scientist, a mathematician, and an author."

2. Select a specific day of the week for "career day." We try to arrange our schedule so that all of our students will be together for the entire day.

3. Let students know the first "career day" they will try out is being an artist. We prepare for "career day" by discussing the different activities an artist might do.

4. Set out art materials that students will need in an "art studio" by placing supplies in different locations around the classroom. We set up areas for drawing, painting, model making, sculpture, collage (cutting/pasting), and crafts.

5. Make a list of tasks for artists to complete during "career day" and discuss these with the class (see figure 17). We ask our students to complete at least three different types of artwork during the day.

6. Discuss the amount of time students have to complete each task. Our students often complete their artwork in the morning, and spend the afternoon setting up displays, looking at the artwork of others, and talking about how the day went.

7. Stop several times during the day and give students feedback on their progress and behaviour. Let them know how much time they have left to complete their work. If students finish early, we ask them to create labels for their displays or write about a piece of their artwork.

8. Give students time to clean up and prepare their displays. We have our students stop working at least one hour before the end of the day so there is plenty of time for cleaning up, setting up displays, viewing, and talking about the day.

9. Have students look at each artist's display.

10. Meet as a class at the end of "career day" and ask questions such as, "What did you like about being an artist?" "What comments do you have for any other artists in the room?"

11. Choose another career for students to experience on another day.

> **Tasks for Artists**
>
> 1. Create different pieces of artwork
>   - ☐ Draw
>   - ☐ Paint
>   - ☐ Model/sculpture
>   - ☐ Collage
>   - ☐ Crafts
> 2. Clean up after working at each area
> 3. Sign each piece of work you complete
> 4. Make a display to show your artwork
> 5. Look at the displays of other artists

Figure 17. Activities for "artists' career day"

Appointments:
setting meeting times to talk with a partner

DISCUSSION

Talking with classmates supports learning. At the end of the year, students use "appointments" to get up, move around, and create personal meaning by talking about their thinking with each other.

STEPS

1. Talk with students about what appointments are and why they are important for their learning. We say, "When you say your thoughts to somebody else, it helps your brain understand what you are learning. During the day, I'll ask you to stop for a few minutes and have an 'appointment' with another person. You and your partner will tell each other what you are thinking."

2. Draw a sample of an appointment page on chart paper (see figure 18).

3. Demonstrate for students how to fill in their appointment page.* We think aloud by saying, "Do you have a space empty at *green*? Would you be my appointment? I am going to write your name on the line beside my *green* and you put my name beside your *green*."

4. Make copies of the black line master on page 57 and give a copy to each student.

5. Give students time to move around the class to set up their appointments. We give our students approximately 2-3 minutes to complete the task (see figure 19). When time is

Appointments

Green_____

Blue_____

Yellow_____

Black line master on p. 57

Figure 18. Sample of an appointment page

Adapted from R. Garmston and B. Wellman

up, we ask the students with empty appointment spaces to come to one area in the room so they can quickly find someone else who also needs an appointment.

6. Give students a specific task to complete during the appointment. For example, after showing a video, we say, "Meet with your *red* appointment and tell each other three facts that you learned from watching the video."

7. Pause at different times during the day to give students time to meet. We use "appointments" during read-alouds, direct instruction, and specific listening times to give students time to think and talk about what they are learning.

8. Meet with students and ask them to give their thoughts about using appointments. To prompt students' thinking, we ask them to complete sentence starters such as the following:

Having an appointment was…

The best part about appointments…

Appointments help my brain…

*Adapted from *Brain-based Learning With Class*

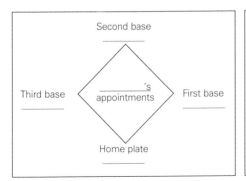

Figure 19. Student set up their appointments

ADAPTATION

For novelty, use a variety of appointment pages such as a baseball diamond, or triangles (see figure 20).

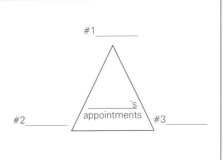

Figure 20. Two samples of appointment pages

Construction Challenge:
using leftover materials in unique ways

DISCUSSION

Involve students in organizing and cleaning up the classroom for the end of the year. We introduce "construction challenge" as a unique way for students to use up the leftover scraps of supplies and materials.

STEPS

1. Explain "construction challenge" to students. We say, "We are going to use up our leftover materials and supplies. To make it fun, I'm going to give you a challenge and you are going to make something unique."

2. Place leftover materials and supplies around the classroom. We set up a central place for tape, staples, and glue.

3. Explain to students that each construction challenge has five parts to complete within a time limit (see figure 21).

4. Give students a "construction challenge." For example, ask them to create a house for an animal.

5. Set a time limit for students to complete all parts of the challenge. We give them approximately thirty minutes for the challenge. We announce when they have ten minutes left to finish what they are doing and have them put away their materials so they are ready to present their "construction challenge" to another person.

Construction Challenge

- ☐ Think about it
- ☐ Make it
- ☐ Name it
- ☐ Show it
- ☐ Talk about it

Figure 21. Five parts of a construction challenge

6. Have students present their construction project to at least two other people in the classroom. We remind our students to tell what they made, what they named their construction, what labels they put on, and any other highlights they want others to notice.

7. Take time to debrief the activity with the class. We ask questions related to the five parts of the challenge such as, "How did you plan before you started making your construction?" "What did you name your construction?" "What materials did you use?" "What labels did you put on?" "What other challenges could we set?"

Figure 22. Students work on their "construction challenge" in class.

8. Have students take their constructions home. Repeat the activity on another day with a new "construction challenge." Some other challenges we use include creating the tallest structure, the strongest structure, a vehicle, something that flies, or something that floats.

Picture Pass:
making collaborative pictures to review themes and topics

DISCUSSION

Working together is a powerful way to review. We have students work in small groups to create collaborative pictures related to topics they have studied during the year. We play music during "picture pass" to help students relax and focus on what they recall.

STEPS

1. Explain "picture pass" to students. For example we say, "I'm going to ask you to draw a picture of something we have learned about this year and you're going to listen to music as you draw. After you draw for a few minutes, the music will stop. That will mean it is time to pass your paper to someone else in your group. When the music starts again, you will add to the picture that was passed to you."

2. Make a list of themes or topics that students have worked on during the year. Post the list and ask the students to suggest other ideas (see figure 23).

Themes and Topics

- water
- rocks and minerals
- elections
- life cycles
- nutrition
- friendship
- pioneers
- measurement
- inventions
- Marie Louise Gay (author)
- Julie Lawson (author)
- Eric Carle (author)
- artists
- butterflies

Figure 23. List of themes and topics worked on during the year

3. Select one theme as a focus for the first "picture pass."

4. Arrange desks or tables so that students can sit in small groups and then give each student a piece of large paper.

5. Select relaxing music to play as students work on their pictures. We stop the music to indicate when it is time for students to pass their picture to the next person in their group (see figure 24).

6. Give students opportunities to do "picture pass" several times during the last weeks of school and use a different topic or theme from the list each time.

7. Decide on a way to display students' collaborative pictures. We place them around the perimeter of the gym at our school celebrations at the end of the year.

ADAPTATION

Have students pass the picture one more time around the group and this time each student labels the parts of the picture they created.

See p. 22

Figure 24. When the music stops, students pass their pictures during "picture pass."

Have a Ball:
taking time to have a break

DISCUSSION

Taking a break is a good way to energize the class or to have everyone pause and relax. Two favourite ways we have our students take a break at the end of the year are "toss and tell" and "invisible ball."

IDEA #1 TOSS AND TELL

STEPS

1. Ask students to sit on top of their desks or tables and tell them they are going to learn a game called "toss and tell."

2. Select a ball that is easy for most children to catch, such as a large sponge ball or volleyball.

3. Ask a question for all students to respond to such as, "What's one thing you learned today?"

4. Toss the ball to one student and when he or she catches the ball, he or she responds. We ask our students to toss the ball back to us each time and when each student has had a turn, he or she sits down.

5. Remind students that they should speak only when they have caught the ball. We also let our students know that each person will have a turn to "toss and tell" so they should not worry about being left out.

6. Continue asking questions and tossing the ball until each student has had a turn to "toss and tell."

Idea #2 Invisible Ball

Steps

1. Have students sit in a circle and tell them they are going to learn a game called "invisible ball."

2. Pretend to take a ball out of a pocket and then show the invisible ball to the class.

3. Go through the motions of throwing the imaginary ball to a student and ask him or her to "catch" it and then "throw it" to another student. We tell our students that we will look directly at the person we are throwing the ball to and they are to look right back at us so we know they are ready to catch it.

4. Remind students that they use eye contact, not voices or sounds, to let someone know they are passing them the "invisible ball."

5. Ask students to throw the ball to people who have not yet had a turn. The game continues until everyone has had a chance to catch and throw the "invisible ball." We ask our students to fold their hands to show they have already had a turn (see figure 25).

Figure 25. A student catches an invisible ball.

Figure 26. Students use up leftover materials in "construction challenge."

See p. 20

Figure 27. Artists c art pieces on "career

See p. 16

INTRODUCTION TO ASSESSMENT

Assessment is information about learning: what is working, what is not, what happens next.

■

Our first goal for assessment practices is to support student learning not simply measure it.

■

Descriptive feedback is what contributes most dramatically to learning.

■

The more students are involved in their own assessment, the more they learn.

■

Students are more likely to achieve goals they set for themselves than ones set for them.

In this chapter on assessment, we offer practical ideas for you and your students to wrap up the school year. Activities include ways to:

■ help students see their strengths

■ have students give themselves feedback

■ interview students about their learning

■ use acronyms as reminders of what is important

■ have students show skills to family members

Can-Do Cards:

making cards to remind students of their strengths

Everyone in the world succeeds best in life when he understands his specific strengths.

— Mel Levine,
The Myth of Laziness

DISCUSSION

Help students recognize the learning they've done over the school year. One concrete way we do this is to have our students identify their own strengths and make a set of "can-do cards." We find this personal record of accomplishment helps students build confidence in themselves as learners.

STEPS

1. Talk with students about how important it is for everyone to know his or her own strengths. We say, "You are going to make a set of cards to show yourself and others some of the things you have learned to do this year in school. When you know what you're good at, it's easier to learn."

2. Record on chart paper a list of skills students "can do." Read the list to students and have them suggest other skills to add (see figure 28).

3. Invite a student volunteer to demonstrate how to make a "can-do card." We ask the

---

Our "can-do" list

I can spell hard words

I can make a pattern

I can add

I can subtract

I can write a poem

I can be a friend

I can play hockey in the gym

I can count to _____

I can read books

I can proofread my work

I can be an artist

I can sing

Figure 28. List of things students "can do"

volunteer to select a skill from the list on the chart paper, record it on the card, and write or draw examples to illustrate how they "can do" the skill. We remind students that everyone is unique and that each person will choose their own examples to show how they can do the skill (see figure 29).

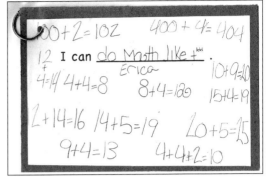

Black line master on p. 58

Figure 29. Student's example of a "can-do" card

4. Make a copy of the black line master on page 58 for each student to complete. We give students several opportunities to work on their "can-do cards" during the last month of school.

5. Give students opportunities to share their "can-do cards" with their peers.

6. Find a way to have each student keep his/her "can-do cards" together. We give our students rings to hold their cards together so they can take them home at the end of the year.

Figure 30. A student writes examples to show she "can do" the skill.

Sign It:
teaching students to give themselves immediate feedback

"Students can effectively monitor their own progress."

— Marzano, Pickering, and Pollock, *Classroom Instruction That Works*

DISCUSSION

Boost learning by increasing opportunities for student self-assessment. One effective and energizing idea is to have students "sign it," or show a physical sign to describe their progress. We ask students to do this while they are working on an activity so the feedback is immediate and students know what to focus on next.

STEPS

1. Talk with students about how their brains need immediate information or feedback to help them learn. We say, "I'm going to teach you a new way to check in and see how you are doing with your work. I'll stop you a few times while you're working and ask you to 'sign it,' or show a sign to give yourself feedback."

2. Make a chart that describes different levels of progress. We use a three level description and include a hand sign to represent each one. This helps both our kinesthetic and visual learners as they connect an image and a physical movement to a description of learning (see figure 31).

3. Demonstrate "sign it" by using a personal example. We might say, "I am trying to keep my bookshelf tidy. If I stop and look at it right now, the sign that I would choose that best describes the progress I'm making is "a little shaky." (We show the sign with our hand). One thing I need to work on next is to put away the paper that does not belong on the shelf."

4. Have students stop while they are working on a task and ask them to "sign it." We say, "Please stop working. I'm going to count 1-2-3 and then say 'sign it.' You will all show at the same time the sign that best describes your progress. After a few seconds, I will say 'thank you' and you'll return to your work."

5. Once students are comfortable using "sign it" to give themselves feedback, help students think about what they need to focus on when they return to work. We pose the question, "What do you need to work on next?" and ask volunteers to give their ideas.

6. Extend the idea of "sign it" by looking at the signs that individuals are showing. Pair up students who show the "shaky" sign with those who show the "high five" so they can help each other. At other times, ask students to find a partner who showed the same sign so they can share what they have done so far.

7. Talk with students about how "sign it" is helping them learn. We pose questions such as, "When I ask you to 'sign it,' what happens in your brain?" "How does 'sign it' help you know what you need to work on next." "What other signs could we use?"

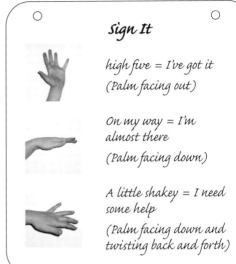

Sign It

high five = I've got it
(Palm facing out)

On my way = I'm almost there
(Palm facing down)

A little shakey = I need some help
(Palm facing down and twisting back and forth)

Figure 31. Chart of three level scale for "sign it"

ADAPTATION

To add variety and novelty, give students three objects; one red, one yellow, and one green to represent the colours of a traffic signal. Students select and hold up the green object to show "I've got it," the yellow object to show "I'm on my way," and the red object to show "I need some help."

Assessment Interviews:
asking students questions about their learning

DISCUSSION

Students can tell you about their learning– just ask them. We have brief "assessment interviews" with each student during the last month of school. This one-on-one time helps students to think about their own learning and, in turn, we often gain valuable insights to include in our year-end communication with families.

STEPS

1. Explain what an interview is and why it is important. We say, "I want to have a special time to talk with each of you by yourself before the end of the year. When we meet, I will ask you some questions and also tell you what I appreciate about you as a learner."

2. Work with students to make a list of independent activities. We pose the question, "What are some of the things you could work on while I am interviewing other students?" We then make a list of their suggestions (see figure 32).

3. Talk with students about ways they can solve their own problems and answer their own questions during interview times. We talk with our

Independent Activities

- read
- write
- draw
- finish work
- use listening centre
- work on the computer
- make a book
- work on my project
- play a board game

Figure 32. List of students' ideas for independent work

students about what they can do when they get stuck, how they can solve problems on their own, and when it is important to interrupt an interview.

4. Prepare student interview questions that will help gain information and insights into their unique thinking and learning (see figure 33).

5. Set aside a space in the classroom for "assessment interviews." To help our learners feel safe and listened to, we sit side by side at a small table in the classroom.

6. Schedule time for interviews. We have several interviews in a day and each one takes approximately five minutes. We focus on listening, and give each student time to think and respond. We also record some of what our students say so we can use their words in our year-end communication with families.

> ## Interview Questions
>
> 1. What are two things that you are good at doing in school?
>
> 2. What is one thing that was hard for you at school this year?
>
> 3. What are some improvements you have made this year?
>
> 4. We've been together all year – what's something about you that I don't know yet?
>
> 5. If I was to write or say something about you, what would you like me to say?
>
> 6. How have you helped make our class a good place to be this year?

Figure 33. List of interview questions

7. End the interview by telling each student one positive and unique thing you noticed during the year. For example, "Wayne, you've been such a good friend to Cliff all year. I notice you help him out when he's having trouble. Thank you."

8. Encourage the class to think and tell about how they used their independent time. For example, we ask "What did you work on?" "If you got stuck or had a concern, how did you handle it?" "What other ideas can we add to our list of independent activities?" We find this process also helps our students be more aware of how they can use independent working time when they are not being interviewed.

Acronyms:
using a word to help students
remember what's important

*"Acronyms…
associate a list of
items in order with
a known word or
sentence, thereby
making them much
easier to remember"*

— Pat Wolfe,
Brain Matters

DISCUSSION

Acronyms are effective ways to provide specific feedback to learners. We use acronyms as one way to remind students of what's important for specific activities and behaviours. The novelty of using an acronym can reenergize and refocus learners. We offer a few favourites to wrap up the year.

STEPS

1. Explain to students what an acronym is and how it can help their brains learn. We say, "There are so many things to remember in school. One way to help our brains remember what we need to do is to use a special word called an acronym. Each letter of this word or acronym reminds us what's important."

2. Write an example of an acronym on a piece of chart paper. For example, we use the acronym TELLS which helps our students remember what's important when they work with a partner (see figure 34).

3. Show how the acronym is a word by circling each letter that makes up the acronym.

What's important when we work with a partner?

(T) alk about the topic

(E) ach person takes a turn

(L) ook at your partner

(L) isten carefully

(S) ay thank you for being my partner

Figure 34. Acronym TELLS helps students know what's important when they work with a partner.

4. Review what each letter of the acronym stands for by asking one pair of students to demonstrate. For example, for the letter *T*, one student can *talk* about the topic, for the letter *E*, *each* person takes a turn, and so on.

5. Reread the acronym with students before they begin the task to remind them what's important when they work with a partner.

6. Offer students feedback during and after the task by telling individuals the letters of the acronym they demonstrated. For example, we point at the letter *L* and say, "Julie and Ajmare, you both *looked* right at each other."

7. Give students opportunities to self-assess using the acronym. For example, we stop students while they are working with their partner and ask them to tell which letters of the acronym they've been able to do, and which letters they still need to work on.

8. Create and use different acronyms to refocus students' attention on what's important (see figure 35).

ADAPTATION

Make a set of large acronym letters. Have the students meet as a class after working with a partner and invite volunteers to select a letter, show it to the group, and give themselves a specific compliment or suggestion for improvement. For example, a student holding up the letter *E* says "Jenny and I *each* took turns."

What's important when we clean up?

W ork together

E verything gets put back in its place

T ime to stop and sit down when the music ends

What's important at free choice reading?

G et a few books and find a space to read

R ead by yourself or with a friend

E njoy your books

A sk some questions

T ell someone your favourite parts and pictures

What's important on a field trip?

O bserve

W onder

L earn

Figure 35. Examples of acronyms

Adapted from *Knowing What Counts: Setting and Using Criteria*

Showtime:
performing skills at home for family members

"We all want that feeling of achievement when we finish something. The best closings elicit an emotional state that celebrates this feeling – the internal reward of accomplishment."

— Eric Jensen,
Sizzle Substance, Presenting with the Brain in Mind.

DISCUSSION

Recognition reinforces learning. "Showtime" takes place at home where students demonstrate the skills they have learned during the year for family members. We find this informal time helps our students end the school year with a sense of accomplishment and provides family members with an opportunity to recognize their child's efforts and progress.

STEPS

1. Introduce the idea of "showtime" to students. For example, we say, "Everyone in this class has learned to do so many things this year. I'm going to ask you to have 'showtime' at home so you can show members of your family what you can do."

2. Make a list on chart paper of skills that all students have learned during the year. Each skill we list is open-ended enough so that every student can successfully perform it at his or her own level (see figure 36).

3. Post the chart and read the list with students. Ask them to suggest other skills they learned in class and add these to the list.

Showtime Skills

- ☐ read aloud
- ☐ do math problems
- ☐ tell stories
- ☐ write stories
- ☐ write poems
- ☐ draw and read maps
- ☐ find information and make notes
- ☐ draw with details
- ☐ sing songs
- ☐ do exercises to music

Figure 36. List of skills for "showtime"

4. Decide on one skill from the list for students to perform for their families. We ask our students to choose a math game they can play with someone at home as their first "showtime."

5. Give students time in class to practice and rehearse "showtime" with a partner.

6. Write a note to families to introduce the idea of "showtime." To make the idea more fun for our students we use invitaton tickets to admit family members into "showtime" (see figure 37).

Dear Families,

You have been chosen to come to a special **show time**. Your child is ready to show you a skill he or she has learned this year at school.

Please set aside a few minutes and decide with your child when and where **show time** will take place.

After the show, please give your child two specific compliments.

FREE ADMISSION TO SHOWTIME

Location: _at the kitchen table_

Day: _Monday_

Time: _7:00 PM_

Feature Attraction: _Sean_ shows how to play a math card game.

Black line master on p. 59 and p. 60

Figure 37. Example of a completed "showtime" invitation

7. Have students invite a family member to "showtime." Together they decide on a time and place for the performance (see figure 38).

8. Bring the class together after they have finished their first "showtime" at home and invite volunteers to tell any "showtime" stories. We ask, "Who did you present to?" "What did your audience tell you they liked?" "What could you do to improve your 'showtime' at home?" "Who is going to be your audience next week?"

9. Choose another skill from the list and have students repeat the steps for another "showtime." We have our students do two or three "showtimes" during the last few months of school.

Figure 38. "Showtime" at the kitchen table

See p. 28

Figure 39. One student shows her "can-do cards."

See p. 32

Figure 40. Teacher holds an assessment interview.

INTRODUCTION TO
RELIABLES

Reliables are ideas that can be depended on to
keep students active and engaged.

■

Reliables are activities that work with a wide range of learners.

■

Reliables offer students choices to show what they know.

■

Reliables let students personalize their learning.

■

With reliables, students know what to anticipate, and
they can say: "Oh, we know how to do this!"

In this chapter on reliables we offer practical ideas
for you and your students to wrap up the school
year. Activities include ways to:

■ engage students in review by using thought bubbles

■ write collaborative summaries of a chapter book

■ take time to play a class game together

■ have everyone respond to a questions

■ use photos to trigger memories

Thought Bubbles:
using a unique way to represent and review

Discussion

Encourage students to try different ways of thinking by teaching them new ways to represent their ideas. We have students use "thought bubbles" as a reliable and effective way to think about their learning, and to review books and concepts worked on during the year.

Steps

1. Explain to students that cartoonists write inside of shapes that look like bubbles to let readers know what a character is saying or what a character is thinking. We bring a cartoon to class to show students examples of "thought bubbles." We also draw two examples on the board so students can see the difference between a "speech bubble" and a "thought bubble" (see figure 41).

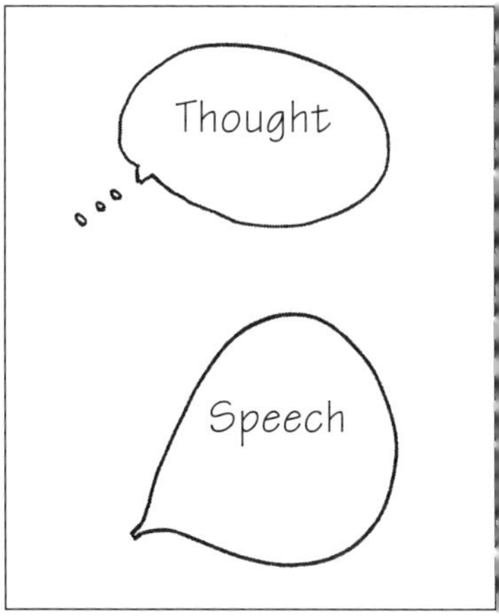

2. Tell students they are going to create their own "thought bubbles." We say, "When a person says something we can hear what they say, but when they just think about something, we don't really know what they are thinking about. You are going to make 'thought bubbles' by writing the words of what someone or something might be thinking."

3. Give students opportunities to complete 'thought bubbles' orally, before asking them to write their ideas. For example, hold up a

Figure 41. Drawings show the difference between a "speech bubble" and a "thought bubble."

picture of an animal and ask students to turn to a partner and say one thing the animal might be thinking. Invite several volunteers to share their "thought bubbles" with the class.

4. Give students practice completing written "thought bubbles." For example, we ask our students to draw a picture of a pet (one they have or one they might like to have) and write thought bubbles to let others know what the animal might be thinking (see figure 42).

Figure 42. A student uses "thought bubbles" to show what her pet is thinking.

5. Bring the class together and ask volunteers to share a "thought bubble" they have written. Students sometimes share advice with the class. For example, one of our students taught the class how to print the thought first and then to draw the bubble around the printing so the words all fit inside.

6. Use "thought bubbles" as a wrap-up experience to review characters in fiction and nonfiction books read during the year. For example, we show the cover and several pictures from a nonfiction book we read to the class, called *Humphrey the Lost Whale*. After a brief discussion, students draw a series of pictures they remember about the story and include "thought bubbles" to show Humphrey's thinking.

ADAPTATION

One adaptation is to have students create "thought bubbles" for inanimate objects as a way to review science concepts such as rocks, plants, and magnets. Or, wrap up the year by having students write "thought bubbles" for objects found in the classroom such as pencils and desks (see figure 43).

Figure 43. A student uses "thought bubbles" to show what his desk is thinking.

Chapter Summaries:
recording and illustrating the big ideas of a chapter book

DISCUSSION

Summarizing is an important skill that supports students' understanding and recall. At the end of the school year, read aloud a special chapter book and have students work as a class to write and illustrate chapter summaries. We make a booklet out of the summaries and present it as a special gift to a class of younger children or to the school library.

STEPS

1. Read a chapter book aloud to the students. We choose a special chapter book to read to our students at the end of the year such as *Charlotte's Web*, by E.B. White.

2. Stop at the end of the first chapter, and pose the question, "What do you think was the big idea in this chapter?" We ask our students to talk with a partner first to give them time to think of a response. After they have talked for a few minutes we have several students share their ideas with the whole class.

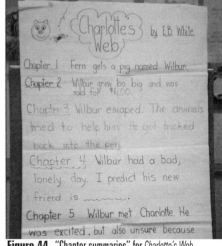

Figure 44. *"Chapter summaries" for Charlotte's Web*

3. Listen to students' ideas and combine them to create a brief summary. Record the summary for the first chapter on a piece of chart paper (see figure 44).

4. Before reading a new chapter, reread the previous chapter summary with the class.

5. Follow the same steps to develop a new summary for each chapter in the book. Record these summaries on the same piece of chart paper.

6. After recording a summary for each chapter, have each student select one chapter summary to illustrate. We have our students draw a picture about the big idea and then copy the chapter summary from the chart paper (see figure 45). When there are more students than there are chapters in a book, we pair students up or have individuals design a cover, write a page about the author, or make a dedication for the book.

7. Bind the pages together.

8. Reread the "chapter summaries" book as a class and ask each student, or pair of students to read the page they illustrated.

ADAPTATION

Students create a "page summary" for a piece of nonfiction writing by recording one or two important facts for each page of nonfiction.

Figure 45. "Chapter summaries" with students' illustrations

Group Games:
take time out for reliable games

DISCUSSION

Even the mention of the word "game" sparks the interest of most students. We introduce reliable games recalled from our own childhoods to give students a chance to slow down the pace as the year comes to an end.

IDEA #1: I-SPY GAME

STEPS

1. Explain the game of "I Spy" to students. We say, "Has anyone ever played a game called 'I Spy?' We are going to play 'I Spy.' One person is going to pick out something they can see or 'spy' in our classroom. This person will give a clue by telling us something about what they are looking at. Then the class will try to guess what the person was looking at."

2. Demonstrate the game to the class by choosing something in the room that is visible to everyone and saying the phrase, "I spy, with my little eye, something that is…" We remind students that when we choose something in the classroom to "spy" it must to be in a place where everyone can see it.

3. Invite the class to guess what is being "spied." Depending on the age of the students, we either limit the number of guesses to five or ask the person to give a new clue so guessing can continue.

4. Continue the game by inviting the student who made the correct guess to be the next person to "spy" an object in the classroom. If no one guessed the correct object, we tell students what it is and invite a volunteer to be the new 'I spy' leader.

5. Increase the challenge of "I Spy" and focus on review of skills by teaching students to use a variety of different clues to identify an object, for example, letter sounds, shapes, sizes, textures, rhyming words, and materials that objects are made of. Our students use a combination of clues such as "I Spy an object made of wood, that is an oval shape," or "I Spy a number that is greater than 17 and less than 50."

IDEA #2: REMEMBER GAME

STEPS

1. Explain the game to students. We say: "I am going to show you some different things on a tray. I will walk around the room once showing everyone what is on the tray. It is your job to try to remember as many of the things as you can."

2. Select a number of objects found in the classroom and place them on a tray. We choose five to seven objects, depending on the age of our students (see figure 46).

3. Walk around the classroom slowly to show students the objects and then cover up the tray.

4. Ask students to try to remember what was on the tray and have them list the names or draw as many of the objects as they can recall on a piece of paper. Give a short period of time for students to complete their list.

5. Uncover the tray and show students the objects, one at a time. If the student remembered the object and listed or drew it, have them place a check mark beside the object on their list.

6. Provide challenge by placing word or picture cards on the tray.

7. Once students are familiar with the "remember game," have a student take on the lead role of selecting items for a tray of objects, walking around the class and then showing the objects one at a time to classmates.

Figure 46. Objects placed on a tray for "remember game"

Sharing Wave:
responding to a question in a unique way

DISCUSSION

Novelty engages attention – especially at the end of the year. Teach students how to do a "sharing wave" as a unique way to have the entire class respond to a question. The activity takes only a few minutes, and each person gets a chance to share his or her idea.

STEPS

1. Talk with students about the "wave" that is often done at sports events and explain how it can be used in school. We say, "Have you seen anyone do the 'wave?' Have you ever done the 'wave?' We're going to do a 'sharing wave' at school where everyone is going to quickly tell an idea as they do the wave."

2. Give students practice doing the action of the "wave," moving their hands up and then down, as they sit in a circle. We talk about how to make our movements look like a smooth wave by making sure one student follows the other quickly so the flow is not interrupted.

3. Ask a question so students can practice a "sharing wave," putting together the action with their verbal response. For example, we might begin by asking students, "What is your full name?" When we ask more difficult questions, we give students the option of saying "skip" if they are not yet ready to respond. Although some students overuse this option in the beginning, we find that most students want to respond and give their idea, especially once they become comfortable with the activity.

4. We use a "sharing wave" anytime during the day when the energy in the classroom is low and we need a way to actively engage our students. We make a list of questions and post these so our students can anticipate how they might respond in the next "sharing wave" (see figure 47).

5. Ask students to give suggestions for what's working with "sharing wave" and how it can be improved.

ADAPTATION

Have students do a "sharing wave" by reading a sentence or two from a book. Or, if students are all working on the same theme or topic, such as spiders, have them do a "spider wave" by having each student read or tell a fact about spiders.

List of questions for "sharing wave"

1. What's one thing you learned?

2. Who is your favourite character?

3. What's one thing you saw on our field trip?

4. What's one fact you found out?

5. What's a good part to read from your book?

6. What picture do you want to show others?

Figure 47. List of questions for "sharing wave"

Photographic Memories:
recording memories of the year

"…you remember it not in words but in images and sounds."

— Pat Wolfe,
Brain Matters

DISCUSSION

Photos conjure up memories. We use pictures taken during the year to encourage our students to reflect and talk about the time they have spent together as a class. Students write memories about the photos and display them for others to see and talk about.

STEPS

1. Talk with students about the power that photos have to help us remember things. We say, "Pictures can help our brains remember things we have done. I'm going to show you some photos of things we did together this year and you are going to think about them and then write down anything you can remember."

2. Display a photograph in the classroom so all students can see it. We place the photo in the centre of a piece of chart paper and ask our students to look at it and think about it during the day so they can talk about it later.

3. Meet as a class and ask several volunteers to tell one thing they can recall about the photo. To help students' remember, we ask: "Who is in the photo?" "Where was it taken?" "What were people doing?" "What else do you remember?"

4. Record what the students say on separate strips of paper. Place these strips around the photo on the chart paper, so they look like a web (see figure 48).

5. On another day, display a different photo in the same spot in the class and ask each student to turn to a partner and tell one thing they recall.

6. Give each student a strip of paper and have him or her print one memory about the photo.

7. Have each student attach his or her memory around the picture to make it look like a web. We invite students to complete as many strips as they can in the amount of time given.

8. Display a new photo on another day and repeat the steps.

9. Use these "photographic memories" as displays for year-end celebrations.

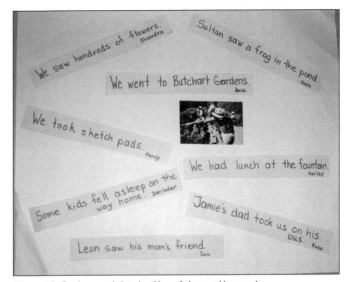

Figure 48. Teacher-recorded student ideas of photographic memories

ADAPTATION

Have students work in small groups and give each group a photo to "web" with their memories (see figure 49).

Figure 49. Students complete their "photographic memories"

Appendix A
professional development

USING THIS BOOK WITH ADULT LEARNERS

The ideas in this book can be used to support professional development activities in different settings; for example, educator's book clubs; team and department meetings and staff meetings; and in-service and pre-service workshops.

Consider the following possibilities:

BRAIN BITS

This idea works well as a way to introduce the book at a staff meeting (where only two or three books might be available).

1. Make a copy of the Brain Bits black line master (page 61) for each participant.

2. Organize the participants into small groups (three or four per group), and have each member in the group do the following:

   (a) Choose a "brain bit."

   (b) Read aloud the quotation to the others in the group.

   (c) Discuss how he/she can relate the "brain bit" to his/her students and experiences in the classroom.

   (d) Invite group members to make comments or ask questions.

3. Have the groups continue until each person in the group has had a turn.

4. Bring all the groups together, show them copies of Voices of Experience, and invite a couple of volunteers to read the books and try some of the ideas with their students.

5. At the next staff meeting, ask the volunteers to discuss what ideas they tried and what they learned.

JIGSAW

Jigsaw is a quick way to introduce the book to the participants. This idea works well at staff meetings or pre-service teacher seminars (when there are large numbers of participants).

1. Divide participants into groups of four. Assign a different section of the book (Relationships, Organization, Assessment, Reliables) to each person in the group.

2. Ask each person to read his/her assigned section and to be prepared to summarize and retell a favourite activity.

3. Each person, in the group of four, takes a turn to talk about his/her section.

4. Invite participants to select one idea that they will try out with their students. Ask each person to come to the next meeting with student samples and stories to share.

BOOK CLUB

This idea works when at least two people are interested in the book.

1. Invite colleagues to form a book club (two or more people make a club).

2. Agree on a time and place for the first meeting.

3. At the meeting, decide how to work with the book. A couple of suggestions: (a) each member reads a different section of the book and selects one activity to try with students, or (b) the group comes to an agreement on one section of the book to read and one idea to have everyone try out before the book club meets again.

4. At the end of the meeting, set a time to get together again. Agree to bring back student samples and stories about what worked, what did not work, and what adaptations were made.

5. Invite participants to record their next steps on a planning sheet (see page 62).

INDEPENDENT STUDY

This idea works well for teachers who choose to work on their own – especially those who are new to the profession and those who are working at a new grade level.

1. Read the book to get an overall sense of its contents (20 ideas for a 20-minute read).

2. Select one or two ideas to try out with students.

3. Use the record sheet to keep track of the idea you have tried, how well it worked, and what idea to try next (see Recording Sheet, page 63).

TAKE ACTION

This idea works well at meetings and workshops.

1. Invite adult learners to try out activities for themselves during staff meetings and workshops. Here are some possibilities:

■ "Good wishes" (page 6)

Make a list of "good wishes" for any colleagues retiring or leaving the staff.

■ "Appointments" (page 18)

At a full-day workshop or meeting, have people set appointments so they have the opportunity to talk to others about their thinking – and to have a chance to get up and move once in awhile.

■ "Sign it" (page 30)

Use "sign it" to have a quick snapshot of progress in relation to topics/issues such as school goals, or a specific initiative.

- "Photographic Memories" (page 48)

  Have staff members web memories around a photograph of a particular school event or celebration. These "photographic memories" can be given as a gift to organizers or school helpers as a way of saying thank you.

Appendix B
black line masters

My name is…

My friends are…

My favourite things to do in class are:

I am proud of…

My special memories are…

I'd like to say…

Figure 2. (page 4)

This Year

All: This year we were learners.

<u>Group 1:</u> Learners who

-
-
-
-

Learners who will keep on learning!

<u>Group 2:</u> This year we were friends.

Friends who

-
-
-
-

Friends who will keep on caring!

<u>Group 3:</u> This year were were readers.

Readers who

-
-
-
-

Readers who will keep on reading!

<u>Group 4:</u> This year we were artists.

Artists who

-
-
-
-

Artists who will keep on creating!

<u>Group 5:</u> This year we were mathematicians.

Mathematicians who

-
-
-
-

Mathematicians you can count on!

<u>Group 6:</u> This year we made memories.

Memories of

-
-
-
-

Memories we will always cherish!

Figure 9. (page 9)

Appointments

Green _____

Blue _____

Yellow _____

Figure 18. (page 18)

I can

Name _____

I can

Name _____

I can

Name _____

Figure 29. (page 29)

Figure 37. (page 37) Outside of ticket

(Note: Photocopy p. 59 and p. 60, double-sided, and cut out as indicated.)

Dear Families,

You have been chosen to come to a special **showtime**. Your child is ready to show you a skill he or she has learned this year at school.

Please set aside a few minutes and decide with your child when and where **showtime** will take place.

After the show, please give your child two specific compliments.

FREE ADMISSION TO SHOWTIME

Location: _____

Day: _____

Time: _____

Feature Attraction: _____ shows

_____.

Figure 37. (page 37) Inside of ticket

1. "The stronger the emotion connected with an experience, the stronger the memory…"

   –Pat Wolfe and Ron Brandt, *Brain Research*

---

2. "Music that you enjoy will cause the release of endorphins – those feel-good brain chemicals."

   –Marilee Sprenger, *Learning and Memory*

---

3. "Emotional stimulation and novelty are two big attention-getters."

   –Marilee Sprenger, *Becoming a "Wiz" at Brain-Based Teaching*

---

4. "It is only in the saying that the learner figures out what he gets or doesn't get."

   –Marvin Marshall, *Discipline without stress, punishment to rewards*

---

5. "Use movement activities to energize students who are at low points in their energy levels."

   –David Sousa, *The Learning Brain*

---

6. "Everyone in the world succeeds best in life when he understands his specific strengths."

   –Mel Levine, *The Myth of Laziness*

---

7. "Acronyms … associate a list of items in order with a known word or sentence, thereby making them much easier to remember"

   –Pat Wolfe, *Brain Matters*

---

8. "We all want that feeling of achievement when we finish something. The best closings elicit an emotional state that celebrates this feeling – the internal reward of accomplishment."

   –Eric Jensen, *Sizzle Substance Presenting with the Body in Mind*

---

9. "Movement …is now understood to be essential to learning…"

   –Carla Hannaford, *Smart Moves*

---

10. "…you remember it not in words but in images and sounds."

    –Pat Wolfe, *Brain Matters*

Brain Bits (page 50)

Planning Sheet

Name: _____

The section I'm focusing on is _____

_____

The idea I'm going to try is _____

_____

_____

Subject/topic/assignment I'm using it for is _____

_____

Time frame: by _____

(date of next meeting)

Comments:

What worked: _____

_____

_____

What didn't work: _____

_____

_____

Adaptations made: _____

_____

_____

Planning Sheet

Recording Sheet	Name: _____	
Contents	**Ideas Tried**	**Comments**

RELATIONSHIPS
  Yearbook
  Good Wishes
  Celebration Scripts
  Thank-You Letters
  Class Songbooks		

ORGANIZATION
  Career Day
  Appointments
  Construction Challenge
  Picture Pass
  Have a Ball		

ASSESSMENT
  Can-Do Cards
  Sign It
  Assessment Interviews
  Acronyms
  Showtime		

RELIABLES
  Thought Bubbles
  Chapter Summaries
  Group Games
  Sharing Wave
  Photographic Memories		

Recording Sheet

Bibliography

Garmston, Robert, and Bruce Wellman. *in conversation*, Vancouver, BC, 2000.

Gregory, Kathleen, Caren Cameron, and Anne Davies. *Knowing What Counts: Setting and Using Criteria*. Merville, BC: Connections Publishing, 1997.

Hannaford, Carla. *Smart Moves: Why Learning Is Not All In Your Head*. Arlington, VA: Great Ocean Publishers, 1995.

Jensen, Eric. *Learning With the Body in Mind: The Scientific Basis for Energizers, Movement, Play, Games, and Physical Education*. San Diego: The Brain Store, 2000.

———. *Brain-Based Learning with Class*. Del Mar, CA: Turning Point Publishing, 1996.

———. *The Learning Brain*. Del Mar, CA: Turning Point Publications, 1994.

———. *Sizzle & Substance: Presenting With the Brain in Mind*. San Diego, CA: The Brain Store, 1998.

Levine M.D., Mel. *The Myth of Laziness*. New York, NY: Simon & Shuster, 2003.

Marvin, Marshall. *Discipline without stress, punishments, or rewards: how teachers and parents promote responsibility & learning*. Los Alamitos, CA: Piper Press, 2001.

Marzano, Robert, J., Debra J. Pickering, and Jane E. Pollock. *Classroom Instruction That Works: Research-based Strategies for Increasing Student Achievement*. Alexandria, VA: Association for Supervision and Curriculum Development (ASCD), 2001.

Sousa, David A. *The Learning Brain*. Thousand Oaks, CA: Corwin Press, 2003.

Sprenger, Marilee. *Learning and Memory: the Brain in Action*. Alexandria, VA: Association for Supervision and Curriculum Development (ASCD), 1999.

———. *Becoming a "Wiz" at Brain-Based Teaching: How to Make Every Year Your Best Year*. Thousand Oaks, CA: Corwin Press, 2002.

Wolfe, Pat. *Brain Matters: Translating Research into Classroom Practice*. Alexandria, VA: Association for Supervision and Curriculum Development (ASCD), 2001.

Wolfe, Pat, and Ron Brandt. "Brain Research." *Educational Leadership*. Volume 56, No. 3, November, 1998, page 13.

Workshops

The authors are available to do workshops on the Voices of Experience series of books. If you enjoyed this book, you'll love their workshops!

Here's what participants are saying:

"Brilliant. Thank you for giving me such wonderful ideas to take back to my class."

"The ideas are easy, inexpensive, and require little preparation."

"Great energy. Wonderful ideas that can be used immediately!"

"Many of your ideas will show up in my class this week. Thanks, too, for the chuckles."

"Thanks, I had fun. I learned a lot and my kids will benefit right away."

"Your ideas help me do the best for my students and still have a life for myself."

For more information, please contact Portage & Main Press at 1-800-667-9673.